Copyright © 2021 Tekkan
Artwork Copyright © 2021

All rights reserved.
First Printing, 2021
ISBN 978-1-0880-0502-6

To contact Tekkan please email:
buddhaboy1289@gmail.com

Table of Contents

of . . . . Page 18

Rest in Peace Mike Finley . . . . Page 33

How to Read My Poems

I want to be direct in my meaning — I want people to clearly understand my meaning. My wordiness is inspired by Shakespeare, and the (aimed-for) concision is in imitation of Japanese style. Using the sonnet with the tanka, I mix the sensibility of the Occident and the Orient — which I have done by living in England, Japan, and America.

I have married the sonnet to the tanka. Often, I don't rhyme my sonnets, because I want freer expression. I tell a story in the sonnet — using three quatrains separated by line spaces, and a final couplet. The story builds to a conclusion in the couplet. The tanka is a commentary, or a counterpoint, to the sonnet — the combined poems have two endings.

Recently I have added limericks, doggerel, and rhymed sonnets into my repertoire. The limericks have a rhyme scheme but the tanka do not.

I don't punctuate much in my poetry. I want the words themselves to do the work. There is logic between words, and the forms provide structure. By not using punctuation I hope to direct readers to carefully attend to each word — to appreciate the graininess of words.

Reading my poems silently and reading them aloud may be different experiences. When I'm not rhyming my sonnets, there's not always a pause intended at the end of the line.

Hint: *unrhymed sonnets are to be recited not as lines but as phrases, and a phrase often overflows the break at the end of a line. I pause and take a breath where it seems natural for me to pause. Another person may pause differently than I do.*

Each poem is a piece of a mosaic, and it is my hope that the collection of poems forms an accurate portrait of consciousness.

My friend, *Will Ersland*, is a wonderful artist. His artwork graces this book.

I am Barry MacDonald. I received the *dharma* name *Tekkan*, which means "Iron Man," a settled practitioner of great determination.

— *Tekkan*

Everyday Mind XXIV

The scarlet of the
sugar maples is
the first to pop.

Benji came to the park for our meeting
In a jacket with fabric around his
Neck with jeans and a ball cap and he does
Appear more bundled up which is fitting
As it is September and it's turning
Colder but then I wonder why he is
Wearing sandals without socks and I quiz
Him on his incongruity asking
Wouldn't his mostly bare feet defeat the
Purpose in choosing mostly warmer clothes?
And he remarks that he's stubborn and won't
Give in to the weather yet which is a
Belligerent attitude I share though
He thinks he is sensible — but I don't.

Cold air and bare feet
make my whole body chilly
but Benji may be
different and through force of
will he can stymie the cold.

On my bicycle gravity gets to
Hurt me on the hill to Houlton when I
Take the strain in my anguished breath and I
Expend the strength of body and heart to
Keep my legs going to raise my head to
Glimpse the crest before I lower my eyes
Because it's much easier not to try
To look above and it is better to
Stay in pace with my shadow on the hill
While my silhouette flexes before me
As my vision narrows as I'm going —
Eliminating stray thoughts is a skill
Moving single-pointedly is gutsy
Defeating the hill is satisfying.

Afterward in the
evening gravity gets to
punish me on the
couch as I recline and then
feel the strain of standing up.

Bison gave the Lakota everything
Said elder John Fire Lame Deer — and we used
His hide for our blanket our coat our bed —
Tipis and drums were made of skin — nothing
Was wasted — at night our drums were throbbing
Alive holy — with his stomach we made
Our soup kettle by dropping in a red-
Hot stone — and his skull with the pipe leaning
Against it was our sacred altar — his
Hooves became our rattles and his horns were
Our spoons — his sinews our bowstrings and thread —
His flesh strengthened us — became our flesh — his
Bones we made into knives — and his ribs were
Our children's sleds — and this is what you killed.

The greatest Sioux was
Tatanka Iyotake
Sitting Bull — when you
killed the bison you killed the
wild natural Indian.

I ask a question of a Zen master
"Where is the pathway to liberation?"
The master flips my expectations
He says "everyday mind" is the answer
At first it makes my footsteps easier
As I can make use of my frustrations
I don't have to strain at self-negation
And don't have to rush to get there faster
Ordinary perceptions are all that
I need as long as I'm attending to
What I am thinking — as it's happening —
The clues are here in what I'm looking at
There's nothing special that I have to do
Even mundane chores can be exciting.

The master says it
is outside of words
outside traditions
and there's nothing you
can do to grasp it.

Of course doing sonnets is just a game
That can't be compared with a hunt for truth
And I do sonnets because in my youth
I got caught up in William Shakespeare's fame
But how I'm doing it isn't the same
Because Shakespeare had to be quite a sleuth
With words without dictionaries for proof
Of the rightness of his words and to name
Phenomena with felicity as
He did far surpasses what I can do
And I'm relying on Rhymzone.com
On the Internet which readily has
So many suitable words easy to
Choose from — which I'm doing without a qualm.

I can't imagine
with my sloppy handwriting
using a pen and
relying on memory
to fashion each of my rhymes.

Imagine using a quill pen trying
Not to make any mistakes knowing that
Each page of paper is precious and that
What a waste it would be to be splotching
Its pristine quality by blundering
With ink and what could one do with a splat
But start over again while feeling flat
And then how absolutely frustrating
It would be to be wasting so much time
In repeating stupidly the same chore
Of attempting not to fumble again
And how would it be possible to rhyme
When the handwriting becomes such a bore
And mindless activity is a drain.

Back in the day the
fops paraded about town
wearing rapiers
which perhaps wasn't so good
for handwriting frustration.

When the sun is coming but hasn't yet
Risen over the horizon the trees
Are only black silhouettes and the leaves
Cast a darkness and it is hard to get
A view of details and the yard is set
In gloom and then slowly the shadows ease
And suddenly a wispy cloud is seized
In a pink light and then the grass looks wet
And drops of dew are shining on the hedge
And the needles of a pine are yellow
And swaths of leaves become brilliant with light
And each angle of the shed has an edge
And a few feathery clouds are mellow
And the sun behind the maple is bright.

A flock of tiny
birds flits between a dozen
trees and most of the
leaves are tinged in a slanting
light but there are still shadows.

It's difficult to talk about issues
With people who aren't attending to the
Small details of politics because the
Public rhetoric is just a tissue
Of lies and the reporters often choose
To take sides and so it's hard to find a
Common ground with people who don't have a
Clue when they put so much faith in the news
Which is tragically skewed — and it's tricky
For politicos because they want to
Be aggressive and not be defensive
And they fashion their lies without pity
For anyone they hurt because it's true
Domination is cruelly offensive.

Ordinary and
innocent people would be
abashed to learn how
many of their opinions
are based upon clever lies.

After the many poems I've written
I think it is possible that the point
Of what I'm doing may be out of joint
With you my readers as I've been bitten
By doing Zen by trying to fit in
A yen for liberation — to pinpoint
The moment of freedom in the midpoint
Of "everyday mind" as I believe in
The saying that each of us is Buddha
But we remain ignorant of the fact
So I am trying not to disappoint
You or exhaust you by leading you on a
Goose chase or by awarding you a sack
Of nothing as if it were a viewpoint.

Walking about on
the hunt for poetic
inspiration I've
been looking for freedom
in the writing of poems.

Genghis Khan was a brutal general
Coming from the steppes of Mongolia
He was the opposite of *Siddhartha* —
Was his vicious cavalry temporal?
Were his gory conquests ephemeral?
He wasn't *Avalokitesvara*
Who is a mythical *bodhisattva*
The Khan's ambitions were imperial —
The horse soldiers of Genghis Khan used bows
And arrows to lay waste to more land than
Any other ruler in history
And his clever brutality was so
Calamitous that his memory spans
Millennia in bloody infamy.

Somehow the hunt for
liberation coexists
with a primal lust
for viciousness that appears to
to be inexhaustible.

If you are one of those who don't turn
To a dictionary when they come to
An oddball word then you won't have a clue
About *bodhisattvas* — so why not learn?
It would only take a minute to earn
A propitious bit of wisdom new
To you on which you could happily chew
Over in your head as it's good to yearn
For a wider circumference of knowledge
And you could also easily look up
Avalokitesvara which I know
Is a puzzle to pronounce on the edge
Of absurdity — but why not shape up
Your vocabulary with some gusto?

You may not know that
Avalokitesvara
is an exalted
bodhisattva who has
one thousand busy hands.

When I got to Aldi's grocery store
I discovered that it was a sad day
Because no matter how much I would pay
I couldn't buy the thing that I adore
Because now they don't have it anymore
And there's really nothing that I can say
And why complain when it is just the way
That things are even though it is a bore
As there is a season for everything
And we have to endeavor to let go
Of succulent items on occasion
Otherwise we risk being ding-a-lings
And suffering is part of life — although
Patience becomes part of the equation.

Now I have something
to look forward to as it's
certain in June or
July watermelons will
be available again.

When the full moon is in the morning sky
It looks like a fixture stationary
Beyond the scattered clouds and it's very
Bright and as I'm absorbing the clouds I
Can see that they're transforming on the fly
As wind-blown wisps moving gradually
And I love to give my sight to airy
Sun lit visions because it breaks my ties
To the drama of my human world that
Never seems to cease for me on the ground
When my thoughts race one after another
But the sky shifts about at a pace that
Dissipates urgency and I'm not bound
To fixate on problems and be bothered.

There is nothing in
the sky to grab a hold of
and give context to
the fact the moon is moving
ceaselessly in an orbit.

Fran said that the swallows are mostly gone
Now and I've noticed that too when I'm on
My bike and so many others are on
The move and Fran says that they're being drawn
Southward not by the increasing cold on
The rise or by the darkness coming on
But because the food that they depend on
Becomes scarce in winter and that they're on
The fly at night so we don't see them go
And may not notice their absence — although
Because my head is in the clouds I know
By association of the outflow
Of the songbirds and I'm sad even though
I know that they'll be back next year to woo.

How can chickadees'
spare muscle and bone
sinew and feathers
withstand the cold of
northern winters?

I returned home in the evening and gave
In to the eventuality of
The season as there does come a point of
No return — in spite of my urge to save
Money — what I felt inside was a wave
Of chilly onslaught which I do not love
So I capitulated and I shoved
A little lever to become a slave
To the thermostat and to my furnace
Once again because I am not like my
Kitcat equipped with fur but am truly
A bare creature and my epidermis
Is prone to the shivers — though I may try
To deny it — the cold facts are ugly.

In Minnesota
the temperature is like
a toothache when at
a definite point we know
that things aren't getting better.

Sometimes I don't know why I bother to
Confabulate with words on paper when
I'm confused and don't know how to begin
But once I get going I do get clues
And the writing becomes a rendezvous
Of amusement and worthiness wherein
My words and humor become a linchpin
In revealing to me what I should do
Because things hold together — or they don't —
And I can waste my time asking "Why not?" —
Which I do regretfully — or I can
Simply experiment with words which can't
Hurt me while I frolic with verbal knots —
And I don't think half-rhyming is a sin.

I'm on a quest to
see how much nonsensical
verbiage I can
slather on a page before
you revolt and stop reading.

of

For some reason he chose the title "**of**"
And I don't know what he was thinking of
And perhaps it was because of his love
Of words that he selected a word of
Little significance almost drained of
Worth except to serve the language thereof
As it does so humbly play the role of
A connection between the words above
Its own articulated power of
Description as opposed to "Molotov
Cocktail" which are two exquisite words of
Incandescent quality with much of
The air of urban revolutions of
Fiery history you may have heard of.

My friend Cid Corman
wrote a two-volume set of
poems of over
1,000 pages with the
provocative title "**of**."

My Mom suffered a spasm of the neck
About a month ago and as she is
Eighty-six years old her condition was
Awful because for days she was a wreck
In terrible pain and we rushed to check
At the clinic with a doctor to quiz
Him about the trouble and to get his
Diagnosis/prognosis with the tech
Of ultra-modern pharmacopeia
And we got some pain-soothing medicine
But mostly our task was to provide care
As now we know there's no panacea
And it's helpful to have a regimen
Of watchful care in which we siblings share.

After a month Mom
is almost back to normal
except that she can't
turn her neck to the right and
so she's not able to drive.

I don't know whether she's my girlfriend or
Not but we've spent a lot of time with each
Other and I believe that she's a peach
And I'd really like to open the door
To a deeper relationship before
Something might happen and she's out of reach
And I aim to be playful in my speech
As I really don't want to be a bore
But I'm only meeting her once a week
Usually at a restaurant and
We talk for an hour on the phone at
Five a.m. and I've had more than a peek
Of her person which stimulates my glands —
I am what am and that's a tomcat.

I have the proclivity
And the creativity
To make her giggle
And then to wiggle
With just my verbosity.

It becomes obvious when a girl gets
Under my skin and starts to bother me
When I'm losing sleep and my thoughts aren't free
When I'm not with her and begin to fret
About her and it's difficult to let
Go and I feel my insecurity
And then I question my maturity
And a part of me certainly regrets
Becoming so damn dependent on her
But when I am with her I go out of
My way to make sure she has what she needs
And I'm shocked at what I do on the spur
Of the moment I think because of love
Which isn't gentle but does make me bleed.

When I'm with her in
a group of people whom I
don't know I don't give
a damn about what they think
and I'll look foolish for her.

This kind of love isn't gentle at all
I do regret my insecurity
I don't like manifesting jealousy
And there are days when I'm in a freefall
When I think that she could be my downfall
As she really appears to be carefree
While I don't know how she feels about me
And I get tired of the folderol
Because I suspect that she doesn't feel
Insecure like I do and she isn't
Losing sleep as I am because I do
Worry that loving isn't a big deal
For her and whether it is she doesn't
Show it — leaving me to simmer and stew.

But then there are times
when our words mesh together
so beautifully that
I am exuberant and
I forget all my troubles.

Of course I have to write about it as
I'm doing my gig of "everyday mind"
And I'm working hard at it — in a bind —
Scrounging for topics with razzamatazz
And love is material with pizzazz
And isn't infatuation defined
As what happens when poise is left behind
When I'm seized by unpredictable jazz
And as love has encumbered my life how
Could I have done anything else but
Grapple with it and put it on paper —
To admit that I may be crazy now —
And to make my insanity clear-cut —
Suggesting that love may be a vapor.

The object of my
love is a person with such
gravity that I
became a moon orbiting
her sunny brilliance.

Perhaps you haven't noticed yet but the
Mind is a wild epiphenomenon
That pops into existence carried on
From continuing vibrations of the
Tiny particles following on the
Cosmic cataclysm still going on
That we have named the "Big Bang" that brought on
Everything out of nothing which is a
Strange phenomenon that's hard to put one's
Finger on and appreciate — and then
You may not have noticed that you have no
Control of so many thoughts — which is fun —
When thoughts just pop into existence when
Least expected at a crazy tempo.

Can you say
what your next thought
will be — and how much
trouble it will cause?

I do scribble about "everyday mind"
Because it's a phenomenon that we
All share and is as simple as can be
And it's not at all difficult to find
But I wonder if I've clearly defined
It enough for you to see how easy
It is not to notice its repartee
For everything that happens is aligned
With "everyday mind" and everything in
The world wouldn't even exist without
Its presence and it's more than the ego
As its fine-woven roots are twined within
Cosmic significance despite self-doubt
As it is consciousness both high and low.

It is the unborn
and undying quality
of consciousness that
exists everyday along
with what is ephemeral.

One of my apple trees is losing its
Bark along its west-facing side and I've
Noticed the branches along the west side
Have been barren of leaves and how sad it
Is to observe my tree going to bits
And I suppose that it's destined to die
Perhaps because the summer was so dry
And there's nothing that I can do to fix
The situation — and I remember
Planting this apple tree because of its
Fruit and its blossoms twenty years ago
With my young family at the center
Of my life — and the tree is on the fritz
And the family dispersed a while ago.

I've adopted the
Japanese tendency
for tasting the sad
transitory nature of
life in the blossoming trees.

What would happen if the idea were
Taken seriously that the thing that
Happens suddenly and the person that
Responds are not separate things but are
Only one happening? Would it be far-
Fetched and such a distortion to look at
The doer and the deed as one thing at
The moment — and would you think that's bizarre?
A poem is happening now and words
Are rising to defined prominence from
A jumble of possible words that are
Subjective and would it be so absurd
To think the poet and the words that come
Reflect cosmic connection that's aware?

It's hard not to get
caught in the idea that
the doer makes it
happen and to minimize
what the cosmos is doing.

I've been exploring Agatha Christie
Paperback murder mysteries that are
On my Dad's bookshelves and the pages are
Yellow with age and I love the intrigue
And so I am reading without fatigue
Because the words that she has chosen are
Perfect for the people and times that are
Vanished now and her plots are so twisty
That I never know what's going to happen
And yesterday I saw on the cover
A fingerprint in what I recognized
As printer's ink and so I was saddened
To realize that my Dad had hovered
Over this novel and was mesmerized.

The printing press that
we both operated
became obsolete
and now the room is empty
except for the memories.

I am incurably curious and
Ask myself questions that I can't answer
And I think the cosmos is a dancer
With the earth spinning on its axis and
Orbiting the sun annually and
With the solar system moving faster
Orbiting the Milky Way — and it's queer
That the Milky Way is moving too and
Going even faster moving away
From wherever the Big Bang exploded —
And I want to face in each direction
One after another but I can't say
How to find each direction within mid-
Air — and these become perplexing questions.

At this moment I am
going in four directions
at the same time —
I want to *know*
the direction
of the earth's rotation
the earth's orbit
the solar system's orbit
and the direction
of the Milky Way.

I am conflicted when I gaze at my
Cottonwood on the corner of my yard
Because it continually bombards
The grass with twigs and branches and they lie
There until I pick them up and I sigh
Because it's troublesome and then it's hard
When all the leaves come down without regard
For my schedule which quickly goes awry
But then I see how fitting the bark is
With its deep grooves for the squirrels to grab
Ahold of and to climb and in winter
The tree's unsymmetrical beauty does
Seize my curiosity in the drab
And frigid season that makes me shiver.

The pure yellow of
the leaves in autumn reminds
me that in China
only the Emperor could
wear the color of the sun.

I am as puny as an army ant
And subject to superior power
Earth rotates at 1,000 miles per hour
I can expostulate and I can rant
But I'm not that much quicker than a plant
Earth orbits at 67,000 miles per hour
Maybe I am a walking sunflower
Unaware of gravitational slant
The solar system orbits the Milky
Way at 500,000 miles per hour
And the Milky Way is very weighty
Speeding at 1.3 million miles per hour
So I am barreling that fast too — *whoopee!*
I'm in the belly of cosmic power.

The speed of light is
186,000
miles per second —
is that quicker
than a thought?

Whenever I think about the future
It won't happen like I imagine it
So why worry even a little bit?
But I think I know what's going to occur
And I concoct my plans as I prefer
Manipulating for my benefit
Thinking of scenarios to outwit
Certain people who I want to deter
But with certain problems I do admit
I can't foresee the snares I will incur
With many outcomes that I won't permit
And I am careful but I only spur
Anxiety — which makes me a halfwit —
Whatever I do the future's a blur.

I'm very clever
and have my best interests
in mind so I am
prepared anticipating —
but it won't happen like that.

Rest in Peace Mike Finley

The sorrow of his daughter's death and the
Disappointments of his life tormented
Him but his misfortunes also sweetened
Him giving his curiosity a
Wicked edge and his vitality a
Biting restlessness which I think he used
To drive his intensity which deepened
Him and I guess that he always had a
Sharp and ridiculous kind of humor
But his suffering gave him sympathy
With the many friends whom he got to know
And as he was a great storyteller
I always noticed his sincerity
Which was a quality that made him grow.

He asked me if I
had children and I replied
that yes I did and
he sincerely suggested
that I simply just love them.

I'm at an age when it is typical
To have known many people who have died
And I think it's helped me to decide
How to be sensible and practical
And feel the emptiness of funerals
To sample the emotions that abide
After the ambitions are set aside
To face the fact of the unthinkable
And maybe my friends will die before me
And few will be left to remember me
Perhaps just several of my family
So it's better to drop my vanity
To be as genuine as I can be
And not be angry — and let things be.

My life will have been
mostly a success if at
my passing those who
know me remember my jokes
and I am not a burden.

At Aldi's grocery store the checkout
Clerks are inquisitive and they inquire
Whether I found the things that I require
And I politely say I've looked about
That I've been careful and hunted throughout
And though I did not tire or perspire
There is indeed something that I require —
I'm not irascible and I don't pout
But there's something to find out about as
I couldn't find my favorite zebra
Or the peppered hippopotamus so
I'm glad the clerk inquired of me and was
Hospitable because it's not the law
And their service is better than so-so.

These clerks don't know how
dangerous and inviting
it is to ask an
open-ended question to
a bored individual.

I am a blasé individual
And my job is to observe politics
To study all about their dirty tricks
And every day it is so typical —
Lying and cheating is continual —
I'd enjoy beating them with whips and sticks
As they're no better than blood-sucking ticks —
And I believe I am forgivable
When I am neglecting what I should do —
Instead of working I'm writing sonnets
Making fun of these political creeps —
If you were me wouldn't you do that too?
They think they're special with glamor and glitz
I've no idea of how they can sleep.

Sanctimony and
righteousness are oh so
propitious for
leveraging a useful
topical accusation.

I used to think that rhyming sonnets was
For the birds because it becomes a drag
And I don't want my poetry to sag
Into feckless stupidity because
I force words together and ignore flaws
While I simply enjoy creating gags
And I do admit that I like to brag
Which consecrating a new poem does
But you should picture me with a sly smile
As I imagine you reading my words
After all this is just mindless fooling
Which I could keep repeating by the mile
So don't blame me if you think it's absurd —
You see it's your time that I've been stealing.

Have you wondered what
the expression "for the birds"
actually means?
Does it imply something is
lofty or ridiculous?

Elliptical orbiting seems to be
A motion that the cosmos loves to do
As even the electrons do it too —
There is so much moving that we don't see
When the planets approach their apogee —
Solstice and equinoxes happen too
The cosmos is dancing a whoop-de-do
And I often forget to say *whoopee* —
But when I notice the sugar maples
That turn into the brightest of crimson
Yellow or orange I can't help but mark
The movement of seasons and I'm able
To cherish the quality of the sun
As the difference of the light is stark.

Scientists discovered
that quarks exhibit
either a left- or
right-handed spin.

Sonnets are a Houdini trick with words
Which I used to think was ridiculous
Because the rhyming is superfluous
Flimflam unless I want to be absurd
Turning rhyming couplets into passwords
So my poetry may be frivolous
Though my intentions are meticulous
But I won't let my essence become slurred
And I am writing sonnets because I
Fell in love with them while waiting for a
Train in Amsterdam while passing time with
Shakespeare's complaints about love and I try
To recapture youthful naiveté
By being a preposterous wordsmith.

I combine
sincerity with
play and confusion
circles into clarity.

Shakespeare lathered on the melodrama
Writing monuments of words about love
And such highfalutin fluff is above
My experience — which is of trauma —
So I'm expanding my panorama
By wanting a woman I'm unsure of
That perhaps I should be more careful of
Because in her own words she gave me a
Warning while we were driving together
The other day saying that the worst that
Could happen would be that we would split with
No further communication — and her
Offhanded comment may become a fact
Of life that I will have to contend with.

The bard wrote
140 sonnets
about an affair
offering no
resolution.

Foolish politicians are sometimes said
To have created circumstances by
Their wickedness wherein they have to lie
And keep on lying with increasing dread
Lest their true character be discovered
As the lust for power intensifies
The magnitude of deceit multiplies
And all they can do is to speed ahead
Deceiving themselves with everyone else
As if they are riding a tiger and
Holding on and being carried along
Lest they tumble off and meet the abyss
Of being eaten by the tiger and
That kind of justice is worthy of song.

Are my own
self-deceits
hypnotic illusions
and snares of love
like riding a tiger?

There was the day at the bagel shop where
I met her for breakfast when she saw a
Table of other guys and she said a
Few of them were datable if things were
Different and I suppose that she cares
About me but there was much more than a
Hint of indifference and maybe a
Dosage of cruelty inside of her
Words which was shocking — and on another
Day we arranged to meet again at the
Bagel place and I waited for her but
She didn't come and so I called her number
And she said she changed her plans without a
Reason — and I was upset — but so what?

Yeah! I think I've
written enough love sonnets
to have fulfilled the
tradition so now I'm free
to address other puzzles.

We don't use quill pens and ink and paper
Any more for the writing of poems
But we do have to have a stratagem
And mine is to stimulate a caper
To have fun and be critical later
By all means not to be *ad hominem*
Especially within a requiem
Where I would be an abominator
But it is my game to finagle words
And to fiddle with a catgut line of
Logic well enough to string a reader
Along skirting the edge of the absurd
Perhaps sprinkling a poem with love
Happy to be a communicator.

I would like to leave
readers with the impression
that I've given them a
a series of bonks on the
forehead with a feather.

Whatever there is to awaken to
The masters who have done it do say that
It can't be seized by force of will and that
There's absolutely nothing one can do
To manhandle its arrival and so
I am lost in a labyrinth of what
It means "to do nothing" to be poised at
A point that only breathing is what I do
And even that is doing something a bit
More than not doing anything as my
Mind is incubating a mess of thoughts
No matter how quietly I can sit
And I'm absorbing so much with my eyes
And with a line of geese I do get caught.

Liberation is
a puzzle as the masters
say the happening
is outside of traditions
and words cannot capture it.

There are so many things to think about
And most of them are just nagging details
As I would like to boost my monthly sales —
I'd like to have fame and money and clout —
Occasional loneliness makes me pout —
Could I be a sailor unfurling sails?
Could I satisfy myself spotting whales?
And how often would I spot a whale spout?
My energy goes into managing
My house and when there are unusual
Disturbances I have to check it out
And yesterday Kitcat was galloping
About and then I heard a strange jostle
And a tapping sound to find out about —
Curiosity is stimulating.

Kitcat jostled the
door from the inside of
the cupboard above
and behind the top of
the refrigerator.

He's a creature of curiosity
And I have underestimated him
Because he can be a creature of whim
Scampering in fits of velocity
Showing animal grandiosity
Which could imply that he's a little dim
But he's very clever with his forelimbs
And surprises me with dexterity
As every morning he waits for me to
Brush him and when I'm through I put the brush
On the floor and he seizes the brush and
Turns it upward and he endeavors to
Brush his furry face himself in a rush
And it's almost as if his paws were hands.

I thought that Kitcat
was only able to brush
one side of his face —
then I saw him turn about
and he brushed the other side!

It happened again at the grocery
Store that another checkout clerk inquired
If I had found the things that I required
And once again I said I didn't see
Just where the hippopotamus could be
And again I saw that I inspired
The disorientation I desired
Which I can use to write my poetry
And then I saw the previous girl and
I told her about my caper and asked
If she wanted to hear my poetry
About herself zebras and hippos and
She did and so we moved off to the side
Where I could become a luminary.

In a corner at
the front of Aldi's I
read my doggerel
about my earnest search for
zebras and peppered hippos.

The maple trees in Japan grow tiny
Leaves that turn a lovely shade of crimson
That I anticipated in autumn
And like the plum blossoms and cherry trees
They are celebrated by Japanese
And over the years I have taken on
Rituals and I am depending on
A mysterious sensibility
To mark the poignant unexplainable
Beauty blossoming and passing every
Season by writing poetry that shows
My appreciation for the maple
Trees that turn such lovely colors every
Autumn on the verge of winter shadows.

The *momiji* trees
are pronounced "momeegee" in
Japanese and once
one has seen them
one always remembers them.

I can't imagine William Wordsworth or
John Keats using the topics that I do
And also worthy Aristotle too
Would object and perhaps even abhor
The déclassé subjects that I adore
But I'm not a fool and I've thought it through
Because "everyday mind" is what I do
Which tells me there's no reason to be bored
With ordinary activity so
Three times a week I stand like a silver-
Back gorilla and heave a 100-
Pound dumbbell up and down and I can go
Very fast because I'm a believer
In exercise — and I'm not an egghead.

I am repeating
a pattern of lines and rhymes
that poets have used
for centuries for fun and
why not be innovative?

The clouds move at a gentle pace across
The sky and every season takes some time
To reach fruition and it's a pastime
Of mine to note the continual loss
Of the autumn leaves that I see are tossed
In the blusters of the wind and sometimes
They fall in batches and at other times
They waft and spiral by themselves and cross
My sight which I savor with a joyful
Melancholy — a sad festival — a
Month of dissolving when the leaves come down
And winter soon arrives and the cheerful
Leftover brilliance of the sun in the
Colors of the leaves lies drab on the ground.

Overcast days and
sharp winds howling through
the barren branches
have about them a bleak
and austere kind of beauty.

I do struggle to meet people where they
Are as I understand that they differ
From me as there are so many fissures
And difficulties getting in the way
Subtle and brutal leading us astray
As if differences were like scissors
Separating us as disbelievers
But we could talk on a happier day
As modern life in America is
Divided by ideological
Poison hyped by the mass broadcasting of
Continual accusation that does
Its best to foster pathological
Hatred — the polar opposite of love.

Differences of
race gender ethnicity
are so needlessly
exaggerated and are
slyly exacerbated.

I knew an intellectual guy who
Was an executive at a think tank
In Washington D.C. with so much swank
One had to have connections to get through
His layers of protection and I knew
Him partially and he wasn't a crank
And he well deserved the highest of ranks
Among thoughtful guys one could bump into
But only in his obituary
Did I discover his admiration
For hippopotami which he expressed
With all sorts of hippopotamus toys
And with obsessional jubilation
Which was not at all what I expected.

I can see that a
hippopotamus is an
ebullient mixture
of weighty pomposity
and impetuosity.

I don't mind being among people who
Have opinions and expectations that
Are opposed to mine but if they are at
Odds with me I'd like to be able to
Talk it through but so often now it's true
It's very difficult to arrive at
A place of neutral ground so to get at
The pivotal issues I look for clues
For flexibility grace and humor
Because I'd enjoy a healthy debate
And I am eager to learn something new
But political divisions are sour
And society is poisoned with hate
So being circumspect is what I do.

Being trapped in the
same room with my poetry
political and
Buddhist friends would become a
delicate balancing act.

If I were to say nothing sensible then I could
Avoid the trap of becoming preachy
And part of me thinks it would be peachy
To publish my books *without words* which would
Be a conundrum to my readers which could
Lead them to believe they were terribly
Cheated so I could be adorably
Quizzical and speculate that we should
Not play the game of believing that we
Ourselves are more tolerant and more
Broadminded than you other people are
As we wallow in our humility
But then I would risk becoming a bore
And whatever I say would seem bizarre.

An empty page
is empty of ideas
and flavorless.

Trimming about the rose bush I got a
Splinter imbedded in my thumb which I
Didn't notice while working to apply
The hedge cutter to daylilies and the
Hostas cluttering the yard which is a
Fall ritual wherein I bend my thighs
And spine to level the slicing blade by
The ground and then to rake and gather the
Leaves I straighten my back not noticing
The unusual strain on my body
And this year I could just pull on most of
The plants and they detached with my yanking
Which was easier than I thought it'd be —
To be done was what I was thinking of.

Leaves are in bags
a splinter's in my thumb
and I didn't notice pain
until I stood and walked.

My friend Jason the ecologist took
Issue with my saying that the trees are
Unsymmetrical pointing out that they're
More exquisitely balanced than they look
Otherwise they'd collapse when they are shook
By the wrenching of the winds and as far
As the spreading branches go they too are
Balanced by the displacement of their roots
So even though there's not a straight line or
A perfect curving form to be observed
There's a subtle composition of poise
Supporting every twist and crook before
The buds of the leaves are prepared to spread
In an epitome of equipoise.

The trees harmonize
with the rotation of the
earth synthesize
with the orbit of the earth
and with the strength of the sun.

Modern people are sophisticated
And with mathematically verified facts
We comprehend both galaxies and quarks
Our disproven theories are updated
Conflicting paradigms are debated
We measure our land with accurate maps
And with nanotechnology perhaps
Utopia is anticipated
While I'm watching the sun as it's rising
Doing my best to imagine that I
Can sense the movement of the earth
That I can feel the horizon moving
And can know the protection of the sky
As if this day were a glorious birth.

It's easier to
notice the pulsation of
my blood and heart and
the swelling the pause and the
dissipation of my breath.

On the corner of my property there
Stands a gargantuan cottonwood and
Now that I've disposed of the hostas and
Daylilies I have to wait and to bear
The dread of the labor to come — to fare
As well as I can — when I take in hand
My rake and lawn bags — when I stand and bend
Shoving the leaves into bags with the flair
That I'm accustomed to — but now I have
To watch and to wait as some of the leaves
Are the brightest of yellow and some are
Pristine green and it is tricky to stave
Off my dread as part of me really seethes —
Which I know to you may appear bizarre.

I bend over and
straighten up for many long
hours and afterward
for several days — because I'm
sore — I waddle like a duck.

Oh! what the tricky rosebush did to me
I thought that I had a thorn in my thumb
Though the day I got it my thumb was numb —
I do not indulge in hyperbole
What the rosebush did was a travesty —
I knew where my prickly thumb came from
I'm really quite clever — I am not dumb —
But I didn't see the reality
There wasn't only one thorn inside my
Thumb but three and so because my thumb was
Numb it took several days to see the truth
Whereupon I seized my tweezers to pry
Them out but I got only two because
Life is difficult — and also uncouth.

The leftover thorn
is there in the middle of
my thumb and I can't
retrieve it and it remains
a nasty provocation.

The leaves are descending gradually
And the forms of the trees are apparent
Their gesturing branches are transparent
The season displays a poignant irony
The way of the world is polarity
Summer days were sweltering — now they aren't —
Nothing upon the earth is permanent
Winter is a time of austerity
But how strange it is that before the leaves
Fall off they turn into the most brilliant
Of colors worthy of jubilation
Before the onset of a winter freeze
And to me the autumn leaves represent
A brief expression of exultation.

Who is it that cares
that everywhere on the
earth rainbow colors
will burst into expression
and then suddenly dissolve?

I thought that I was through with her and then
She called and apologized giving me
A story about being suddenly
Despondent and full of self-revulsion
And when that happens there's a compulsion
To sympathize with female company
She said and she called Donna and Sherry
And they went shopping and later on when
She realized that she left me hanging
Waiting for her she said she was sorry
And she wants me to forgive her again
As this is a time when she is hurting
And she's not angry at men — like Sherry —
And she knows that I understand her pain.

I marvel at how
she maneuvers me into
a position where
she neglects me and then she
plays upon my sympathy.

I haven't been angry with her after
All the things she's put me through — at least not
In her presence — but she's tied me in knots
Of frustration which I haven't shown her
And she's very difficult and she spurs
My perplexity now that I am caught
Between attraction and being distraught
Which I cannot let happen forever
Because I'm waking up in the middle
Of the night unable to quiet or
Divert my mind from her and getting up
Doing Zen still leaves me in a muddle
Which means that I have to do something or
Else go on being nervy and screwed up.

I had a taste of
being relieved of tension
and uncertainty
so maybe I can try some
purposeful indifference.

I can see how the monks of Asia would
Separate themselves from the tangles of
Ordinary life like romantic love
Because it's much easier and how could
One follow the allure of womanhood
And liberation also — so full of
Conflicting perplexities are both of
These paths — and yet I think it would be good
In each case if I could learn to relax
When I would like to — and when I need to —
Because so often my emotions run
Away with me inflicting painful cracks
In my composure and knowing what to
Do is easier when I'm having fun.

Surely with either
romantic connection
or a Buddha kind of
of liberation things would
come easier with a smile.

Rhyming sonnets is only a game that
I play and in choosing my words I make
A spontaneous bet and so I take
A real risk with my time and effort that
I can find a harmonious word that
Rhymes and that also pleases for the sake
Of rhythm and sense as it's a mistake
To focus narrowly and to fall flat
With the poem's overall impact as
Reciting a poem is like telling
A joke and if the punchline doesn't work
If there isn't any razzamatazz
And then if I look like a ding-a-ling
My handiwork fails — and I am a jerk.

There is such fun in
the spontaneity of
seizing on a word
and mixing it with other
words to make a quirky joke.

At the top of an ash tree I saw a
Couple of crows and the leaves were down at
The very top but were holding on at
The middle and the crows perched apart a
Little distance silently and then the
Crow on the right bobbed and cawed and then the
Other bobbed and cawed in a manner that
Suggested they were irritated at
Each other tangled in some sort of a
Disagreement and were sniping at one
Another in the way that couples do
And I thought what a dreary scene it is
And how powerful it is when one shuns
The other — and even animals do
It too — and how depressing it all is.

After a passage
of silence and sniping the crows
departed and flew —
together — leaving the tree
to shed its remaining leaves.

I am going on with the idea
That I have my sensual faculties
And my various attitudes and these
Are my determining phenomena
And — because of my dipsomania —
I believe that I can't do as I please
Can't indulge every urge that I am seized
By and if there is a panacea
It's what I can do with my attitude
And I realize I can't wrench myself
Into a better way of feeling but
That I can with a practiced latitude
Let go — as any emotion in itself
Is fleeting and need not become a rut.

If I'm able to
gently coexist with my
perplexities and
frustrations they will simply
dissolve — eventually.

Very often with groups I've been part of
It seems I'm on the outside looking in
And emotions arise that are akin
To aversion with the loneliness of
Being apart and with the confusion of
What to do to quell disruption within
That leads me to self-justification —
When what I want is acceptance and love —
But it does me no good to run away
From such puzzles and I think that it's good
Practice to see what happens over time
To discover whether there comes a way
For harmony to arise — so it would
Be best to be patient in the meantime.

I do have to live
with painful paradoxes
with abiding faith
that I don't have to impose
a forceful resolution.

You may have noticed that I am seeking
Enlightenment by writing poetry
Which maybe is conceited lunacy
As I'm taking pleasure in exploring
Sensuality and in detailing
Ordinary events with clarity
Fixing on the potentiality
That happenstance may be conspiring
With way-seeking mind and I admit I
Can't grasp liberation by force of will
And the harder I try the less likely
I am to succeed — but shouldn't I try
As there is a chance? And maybe I will
Grasp what can't be grasped — at least consciously.

I would like to be
surprised by events into
a revelation
so I'm patiently waiting
and expecting a surprise.

The great gift of Sunday is that I don't
Have to do anything that's scripted by
My livelihood and that I set aside
Regular exercise and I don't
Feel guilty about it because I won't
Let my morning relaxation go by
Without easeful meditation to ply
Thoughts to carefree exploration so it's
Propitious to sit and linger at
My keyboard looking outside the window
As I am fishing in the air for words
With open childlike expectation that
If I wait — even though I don't know how —
Cheerful exuberance comes with my words.

Once I've exhausted
my perceptive energy
my satisfaction
allows me to do household
chores with a happy éclat.

I could be expending effort building
An intellectual superstructure
Weaving philosophical contexture
With metaphorical might resembling
A Gothic cathedral of soaring
Thought anchoring objective conjecture
With flying buttresses as a lecture
Of perfectibility humoring
My conceit with a lofty angled vault
Raised above an expansive lonely nave
Exquisitely enlightened with stained glass
Consistently eliminating faults
Believing myself to be very brave
Becoming an intolerable ass.

I can't live without
a reliable point of
view and while it's good
to be consistent I know
my thoughts are perishable.

I don't have or want a publisher
As I am publishing my books online
And edit exhaustively every line
Rereading every page five times over
And I am determined to do over
Any defective poem taking time
Thinking that any mistake is a sign
Of carelessness and so I look over
My books when they arrive and yesterday
While flipping through the pages I noticed
That one poem was a line space too high
On the page and saw I was betrayed
With a slighting of my *magnum opus*
By a laxity that escaped my eye.

However much I
finagle whatever I
do there seems to come
a moment when a puncture
lets air out of my balloon.

I wonder if a repeated pattern
Of words for example rhyming sonnets
Has intrinsic value or whether it
Is just an ego-based foolish concern
As a sassy display of skill to turn
A phrase in any direction to fit
The predetermined form showing off wit
Which at bottom is about self-concern
But I get bored easily and don't want
To write about the same things over and
Over and to keep going I want to
Answer questions and I don't want to flaunt
Verbal dexterity uselessly and
There is always more exploring to do.

I want to bump up
against the vague edge of the
inexpressible
and for that I'm going to need
much verbal dexterity.

A group of us have come to Pioneer
Park for a gathering which overlooks
The river valley with the dawn in flux
With light on the verge ready to appear
As the beauty of the day is austere
As the season is approaching a crux
Growing colder and darker in redux
Of a seemingly barren season near
Again but we have a portable fire
And we each have a time to say our piece
About experience not feeling drear
In our hearts and our meeting does inspire
A satisfying talk that does bring peace
That gives to the season a certain cheer.

A guy lingers on
the edge of tears wanting
not to break down
talking about memories
of deer hunting with his dad.

When I meditate I make an oval
With the fingers of my hands which rest on
My lap and sometimes I will dwell upon
The oval of my hands as a focal
Point and as my body is immobile
My hands are an epiphenomenon
And my whole consciousness is resting on
The oval space within my hands and so all
My thoughts are arising within my hands
And I hold the force of my life the flow
Of my energy in my hands the fire
Of my attention rests in my hands and
The beating of my heart and the bellows
Of my breath feed the air to my bonfire.

When I finish with
meditation and I move
about doing my
business I have a buffer
between me and disturbance.

The cottonwood on the corner of my
Property is a power unmindful
Of my preferences and I am fretful
Of the coming cold and every year I
Do try to mulch or to bag the entire
Dispensation of all its leaves careful
To finish before the snow comes grateful
To have my yard looking tidy so I
Don't have to do an autumn chore in the
Spring so that I watch the days go by and
I see and wait for the yellow leaves to
Fall but there is nothing to do in the
Meantime but to quell my impatience and
Linger until the heaps of leaves accrue.

The yellow flags of
cottonwood leaves turn and
reflect leftover
summer sunshine and once they
go the landscape becomes drab.

OK I have reached the point in the book
Where I am going to dispense with rhymes at
Least at the end of my lines but I'll be
Counting syllables and measuring the

Length of my lines and the task of writing
Remains the same that is to compose the
Right words in the correct order without
Wasting space on useless words that are there

Only to make a ten-syllable line
With the overall purpose of leading
Up to an ending that is worthy of
The writing and the reading of it for

Otherwise I'd let you down and you could
Languish in a dystopian cosmos.

The world is pregnant
and poignant with meaning and
I hope some of it
emerges in word tracery
upon these empty pages.

My elderly Mom is assailed by a
Telephone fraudster who frightens her with
His claims of government authority
Declaring her Social Security

Number is compromised and that to catch
The thief she needs to go to Walmart and
Walgreens and to buy $500
Gift cards and so by reading the number

On the back of the card to the caller
She could be protected from this scumbag
Which is a damnable lie repeated
By this insolent slimebag ensconced in

A lair somewhere in America who
Preys on the fears of the elderly.

Disconnecting my
mother from the phone is not
a solution but
persuading her to hang up
ferociously is helpful.

Across the river valley in plain sight
From Pioneer Park there stands a tower
With antennae for cell phone coverage
And before dawn lights are blinking on the

Tower a glowing lovely scarlet flash
Timed with intervals calculated I
Am sure to catch the attention of a
Nighttime pilot and everything about

The tower is a technical achievement
Of the modern age but in the darkness
I am able to gaze at the winking
Light with childlike rapture that thrills with such

Simple delight in the beauty of things
Apart from my dull rationality.

Down the valley and
two miles away the Crossing
Bridge is festooned with
emerald and ruby winking
lights shining upon water.

It's in our literature and is part
Of our lore that we compulsive drunks will
"Intuitively know how to handle
Situations which used to baffle us"

After we've been revived enough for the
Anesthetized fog of euphoria
And of despair and then of hangovers
To have dissipated and then even

Into sobriety the tangle of
Emotion that fuels a drunk must be faced
And allowed to dissipate after which
The frustrated and agonized love that

Lies buried within us for many years
Finds enough freedom for its expression.

The expression of
loving understanding we
see and hear in
our faces and our voices
is what we give each other.

On any day I have only to look
Up from my keyboard while I am busy
Collecting my thoughts to observe through the
Window that on certain days the sky is

Heavy with clouds casting a gloom upon
The earth and on other days a few clouds
Will be moving sometimes to the south or
To the north with a unique difference

Of touch every day and today there are
Very few clouds and the remaining leaves
Are bright with yellow light and feathery
Wisps of the clouds are speeding southward with

An awe-inspiring drama as I
Can see their brilliant whiteness transforming.

They lead me to think
of the sail-rigged and sleekly
designed clippers full
of lusty sailors plying
skills on the swelling ocean.

I ruined my handwriting doing a
Lengthy freshman essay in college by
Writing in a rush compulsively as
I struggled to keep up with the blasts of

My thoughts and ever since then even though
I try to be careful I am sloppy
So it's good to use a computer for
Poetry and now I sit and dwell with

Thoughts before I strike a key as I am
Not scattershot anymore but I do
Have to use a pen when thanking people
For their donations to my business and

Handwriting is a peculiar kind of
Labor with such convulsive hand fatigue.

Occasionally
I exert effort to write
every letter of
"Parkway" but usually
I just scrawl "Pkwy."

Aristotle preferred elevated
Topics for poetry and so I guess
He'd take a low opinion of my lines
As I take an interest in the little

Red squirrel that runs along the top of
The white fence in the yard outside of the
Window and I'd like you my reader to
Watch with me with simple pleasure as the

Squirrel follows the curving pattern of
The fence scampering up and down stopping
And resuming turning a corner and
Disappearing behind a shed and with

Me perhaps you may lighten your mood and
Escape the nonsense you were thinking of.

Observation of
ordinary happenings
may well become a
pleasurable relief from
embroiled preoccupation.

I was new to the poetry reading
Scene and he had made an impression on
Me as being a poet who knew what he
Was doing so I summoned my courage

And laid before him the seven books that
I self-published and he was courteous
And kindly praised my daughter's cover art
Which gave the books harmonious appeal

He said but then he remarked that it's hard
For poets and that we poets often
Can't even give our work away and I
Believe that night he recognized in me

The hungering ambition to become
Through force of will somebody important.

At our monthly show
the "Barbaric Yelp" on a
depressing winter
night Mike Finley was hurting
from chemotherapy

I left the "Barbaric Yelp" that gloomy
Night feeling like an outcast which I'm sure
Was not Mike's intention and then I bumped
Into him at many venues about

The Twin Cities where he introduced me
To his friends and he gave me a welcome
Access to his home his conversation
His experience — with the lessons learned —

And as one of his friends I was grateful
To shelter under the umbrella of
His compassion which he spread above the
Many people whom he got to know and

Mike has served us as a guide because
He had suffered and rejoiced so deeply.

Many friends at his
memorial told stories
of youthful ribald
explosive optimistic
and verbal exuberance.

A friend of mine related how he liked
The female attention he received from
The young nurses who cared for him in the
Hospital after colon surgery

And he reminisced about his father
On his deathbed in the hospital when
His Dad confided that even on the
Threshold of death he was attracted to

The fetching young nurses about him as
If he were a 30-year-old able
To seek a woman again and I groaned
With the recognition that as long as

My heart circulates blood I will never
Be free of the desire for women.

I could believe that
this overwhelming yearning
is an affliction
or that it's God's blessing but
I can't be indifferent.

The sparrows are playing flitting between
Several trees as a roving flock and
They dip in flight and rise before they perch
And they turn suddenly in the air toward

Another tree and they're not flying in
Formation purposely as the geese do
But are frolicking restlessly at ease
Hopping and perhaps hiding however

Temporarily in the remaining
Foliage and the sparrows aren't giving
Any thought to their acrobatics as
Nothing could be easier than flight and

Busybody scavenging in a group
For them as they move to different trees.

They rise together
above the trees swerving
and darting away
leaving the increasingly
bare branches to twig gestures.

I turn the corner in my car and see
The oak trees that are three blocks ahead that
Mark the place on the street across from my
Office which is a view embedded in

My daily routine hardly worthy of
Notice yet the oaks which are the last of
The trees to shed their leaves are well into
Autumn and the leaves are shining in a

Poignant red in the morning light that brings
To mind a morning of the previous
Winter of the sight of frost-encrusted
Bare branches glowing within an orange

Brilliance transiently before the sun
Moved on and then the light dissipated.

The distinctiveness
of oak leaves and oak branches
do assert themselves
periodically in my
mind in my yearly routine.

For 25 years I've made disposing
Of the cottonwood leaves that fall on my
Yard a much bigger chore than it needed
To be by waiting until all the leaves

Were down thinking as I did that it is
Better to do all the work at once and
Be done with it but this year I have mulched
With the mower as leaves landed over

Several days and they didn't have the
Time to accumulate in odd places
On the patio and betwixt the house
And garage so I didn't rake so much

So that I didn't have to bend over
To bag the leaves which does make me so sore.

Only in retrospect
after blundering into
different ways did
it emerge that it's not the
time but the strain that matters.

As I was removing my friend River's
Wheelchair from the trunk of my car a round
Blue bottle of bug spray fell from a bag
That was slung between the handles of the

Chair and it hit the asphalt plopped and broke
Into shards of glass that scattered about
And River had forgotten about it
And didn't mind its loss and I knelt to

Observe the variously sized and sharp
Pointed bits and with the rounded tips of
My fingers I collected the larger
Pieces and placed them on a little wall

And then being delicate I lifted
Tiny shards and put them into my palm.

I collected the
shattered bottle in one
hand and dropped it in
a dumpster nearby without
slicing or pricking fingers.

I try not to think about it because
Looking for it hinders the happening
But the shock of the breaking of the blue
Glass bottle may be a symbol of the

Moment when delusion vanishes and
A realization of reality
Arrives and the body and mind are thrown
Off and Buddhist enlightenment is in

Hand but that didn't occur for me — much
To my disappointment — so I did the
Essential thing that I could do which was
To patiently and to wholeheartedly

Collect the sharp bits — careful not to pierce
My fingertips — not to puncture my palm.

As I understand
it even the slightest thought
embedded in my
mind — that I have to grasp it —
will prevent liberation.

I would like you my reader to get my
Metaphors with alacrity without
Having to make vague guesses as it is
My gig to look for extraordinary

Ridiculous insight in everyday
Things or — in other words — ordinary
Magic and so I should warn people and
Friends that I'm literal when putting words

Together and if you live within the
Circumference of my consciousness then
There's a possibility that you will
Become an epiphenomenon — that

What you do may be memorialized —
Because I'm looking for material.

With the exception
of a girlfriend on the verge
of becoming an
ex-girlfriend most people don't
know that I am watching them.

If you have a hankering for putting
Words on paper maybe for reasons
You don't yet understand knowing only
That it's exciting to express yourself

To clarify what's important or to
Uncover sly emotions disguising
Genuine emotions or that you have
Stumbled on the secret — that the act of

Writing brings out buried treasure that you
Could find in no other way — if these things
Are true for you then you should create a
Sanctuary in the day for writing

And arrange your routine so that you are
Most awake and alive during that time.

If you have done so
much as to have established
a sanctuary
then the writing becomes a
habit not easy to quit.

Imagine who is reading the writing
Even though at the moment it may be
True as Mike Finley said that poets can't
Give their work away — imagine that the

White page with your words is touching the thoughts
Of someone who's open and eager to
Be a partner — maybe not indulgent of
Your self-pity moroseness — but yet one

Who is not as harshly critical of
You as you often are of yourself — and
Believe that the one you are writing for
Comprehends admires and loves you — and

If you can do that then the words will find
Harmony and you will become happy.

Imagination
can transform the writer's fear
of the empty page
into an unshakable
ever-present companion.

Gripping twisting and pulling with enough
Pressure to accomplish my purpose is
What I sometimes have to do in the course
Of using tools and getting things done and

I'm focusing strength and thinking only
Of results and at other times I am
Striking the keys of the keyboard watching
Letters emerging in rows on a screen

And my fingers are disciplined with years
Of training and are invisible to
Me in a perfunctory way of thought
But I'd like to explore you with touching

Holding and caressing delicately
Consciously with the tips of my fingers.

As if they were the
hands of a child again I'd
like to explore with
you exquisite textures with
loving receptivity.

It is nice to have a garage for a
Car when the first frost of the year sticks to
The windshields of the exposed cars and has
To be scraped off with an edged tool with strength

As I don't have to do that anymore
But I remember the years when I gave
Space to my then-wife for her car and the
Memory is sweetly regretful that

No matter our one-time intentions we
Are better off apart as I see the
Roofs of houses coated in the frost and
The cold of the air penetrates my lungs

And breathing is a little burdensome
As I wait for warmth from the car's heater.

It is nice to have
someone to make such little
sacrifices for
and in their absence the good
deeds done are sweetly missed.

If I keep my eyes open the lag of
A season can take my breath away as
The calendar days go by and I see
The daily demarcations pass in a

Gradual sinking of temperature
In the slow emergence with touches of
Color in the leaves in the selection
Of the heavier clothes that I wear but

I'm watching the trees outside the window
In the absence of a wind dropping their
Leaves fluttering straight down by the hundreds
At a steady pace and in the little

Time it takes to assemble these words the
Stark aspect of the bare branches appears.

Suddenly squirrels
have nowhere to hide and the
valley beyond the
homes and trees is visible
and will be for the winter.

There is the turn every day when I'm done
With the poetry preceded by the
Meditation informed by a hunt for
Liberation when I attend again

To the daily news as a partisan
And because I've been doing this for a
While I can gauge the predatory moves
The dishonesty of political

Talk and the contempt propelling so much
And I believe the world is better off
Because I do political writing
Wherein aggression is expected and

Rewarded — but at the same time I am
Balanced with roots in the ethereal.

Oppression is a
fact counterbalanced by
little expressions
of love persisting throughout
redeeming our intentions.

Fortunately — I have my wits about
Me so that I can cruise smoothly into the
Future while satisfied imagining
What it will be like luxuriating

Rehearsing memories being able
To cherish productive years relishing
Well-earned pride in a compendium of
Poetry wherein reading each of my

Poems will recall to me moments of
Happy exploration involving a
Web of circumstances and connections
And companions wherein I will need to

Overlook the maladroit expressions
That eluded my proofreaders and me.

A sour thought intrudes
reminding me that
whatever I think
will happen — it won't
happen like that.

It has happened so frequently once I've
Confirmed a recognizable profile
Of a female who lives overseas as
A Facebook friend that she encumbers me

With text messages initiating
A whirlwind romance professing as she
Does that she's been treated horribly and
She wants sincerity integrity

And love and she offers fetching photos
Of herself gorgeous and decades younger
Than me and she eagerly awaits my
Response ensnaring me in dialogue

Devolving perhaps to impatience with
My hesitancy to send over money.

Who's titillating whom?
as usually I don't
allow the game to
start as the question becomes
who will be frustrating whom?

The scarlet maple
leaves are grounded — the sun
crests the horizon.

—*Tekkan*

www.ingramcontent.com/pod-product-compliance
Lightning Source LLC
Chambersburg PA
CBHW051551010526
44118CB00022B/2660